T0129322

A Genealogical Diary and Autobiography of David Michael Latouche

DAVID M LATOUCHE

authorHOUSE®

AuthorHouse™
1663 Liberty Drive
Bloomington, IN 47403
www.authorhouse.com
Phone: 1 (800) 839-8640

Published by AuthorHouse 06/19/2018

ISBN: 978-1-5462-4591-9 (sc)
ISBN: 978-1-5462-4592-6 (hc)
ISBN: 978-1-5462-4590-2 (e)

Library of Congress Control Number: 2018906712

Print information available on the last page.

Contents

Dedication

I have written my personal diary and autobiography in memory of my dear and departed mother, Mary Maxine Roome (maiden name).

Even though I never had the pleasure of knowing her, I have been told that her greatest desire was to write her story.

Since she wasn't able to achieve this, I am making an effort to gratify her desire by explaining how I came to be while honoring both my father, Galen Arthur La Touché and my mother, Mary Maxine Roome, whom I surely would have loved so very much, if I had been given the chance.

From having been a ward of the courts and the State of Indiana, upon my birth, and being placed in to foster homes, orphanage home including state mental institutions during my younger years.

I experienced many frustrations of not knowing who, where, or was my natural family.

Notice

This book may not be reproduced in whole or in part, or stored in a retrieval system, or transmitted in any form or by any means – for example, electronic, mimeograph, photocopy, and recording – without the prior written permission of the author.

A Note To The Reader

The illustrations, pictures and text written in this book are based on actual facts from documentation that has been recorded through the years.

Prayer

Help Us, O' Lord Whenever We Sort Through Our Thoughts, Evaluate Our Living, Examine Our Purposes, Face Our Doubts and Discover the Support of Your True Love, to See Better Where We Fit In to the Whole Picture of Your Will and Kingdom.

Through Jesus Name We Pray, Amen

Preface

There are many reasons why I am writing my personal diary and autobiography but the most important one is in hopes to stipulate the importance of how cruel and insensitive life can be when a member of a family is taken away. This story is not only true, but it is based on actual documentation of the first twenty-one years of my life.

I firmly believe that each and every person should be entitled the "Right-to-Know" their origin, "regardless-of-any-situation" and the out come, should they desire? By the same token I believe that everyone should be accountable for themselves and what they produce.

My story consists of many hardships, and punishments including being raised in foster care homes, orphanages, juvenile detention center in Indianapolis Indiana until my thirteenth year.

During my younger years of adolescence, and teenaged years, I became accustomed to repeated abuse and neglect that caused me to eventually suffer from post traumatic stress disorder through my depression years.

Biography of My Father, Galen Arthur La Touché

My father, Galen Arthur La Touché, was born October 11, 1924, in Concord, New Hampshire. He was the child of Arthur La Touché and Ester Mae Powell.

Galen served in the US Army from April 12, 1943, until February 17, 1946, and he received an honorable discharge as a duty sergeant.

My father's service record indicates that he served in the Battle of Luzon and in New Guinea during World War II, and received the Victory Medal, the American Theater Campaign Ribbon, the Asiatic Pacific Theater Ribbon, and the Bronze Service Star.

Following my father's discharge from the armed forces, he married my mother, Mary Maxine Roome, on August 30, 1947.

I was able to meet up with my father in August 1979 when he attended the Fayette County Country Fair as an exhibitor.

After meeting up with my father, I visited him while he was living in a small trailer with his second wife and daughter, where he told me that I also had a brother named Christopher Arthur La Touché, who was working for Reithoffer Shows.

While I was visiting my father, I learned that the stories that were told me by my mother's family were just stories to be told and they were not the same stories that my father told me. So I confronted my mother's sisters after returning to Indianapolis.

This caused them to become angry and frustrated at me. My mother's family said that they no longer wanted to be associated with me and began judging me because of the places and people I acquainted myself with during my homeless years.

Shortly after arriving, I lost my father's contact information, which I had written down in order to remain in touch with him. My father died at the age of sixty-one, leaving his son Christopher Arthur La Touché and daughter; he died on December 5, 1985, in Bowling Green, Warren County, Kentucky.

Family Record

NAME: <u>GALEN ARTHUR LA TOUCHÉ</u>

BIRTH: <u>OCTOBER 11, 1924</u>

GENDER: <u>M</u>

PLACE: <u>CONCORD, NEW HAMPSHIRE</u>

RACE: <u>CAUCASIAN</u>

MARRIAGE: <u>AUGUST 30, 1947</u>

PLACE: <u>INDIANAPOLIS, INDIANA</u>

AGE: <u>22 YEARS</u>

DEATH: <u>DECEMBER 5, 1985</u>

AGE: <u>61 YEARS</u>

INTMT: _____

PLACE: _____

FATHER: <u>ARTHUR LA TOUCHÉ</u>

MOTHER: <u>ESTHER MAE POWELL</u>

Father's Certificate of Discharge

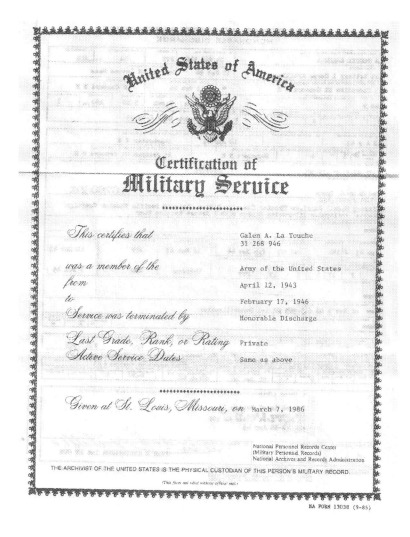

United States of America

Certification of

Military Service

This certifies that

Galen A. La Touche
31 268 946

was a member of the

Army of the United States

from

April 12, 1943

to

February 17, 1946

Service was terminated by

Honorable Discharge

Last Grade, Rank, or Rating

Private

Active Service Dates

Same as above

Given at St. Louis, Missouri, on March 7, 1986

National Personnel Records Center
(Military Personnel Records)
National Archives and Records Administration

THE ARCHIVIST OF THE UNITED STATES IS THE PHYSICAL CUSTODIAN OF THIS PERSON'S MILITARY RECORD.

(This form not valid without official seal.)

NA FORM 13038 (9-85)

7

My Father's Death Certificate

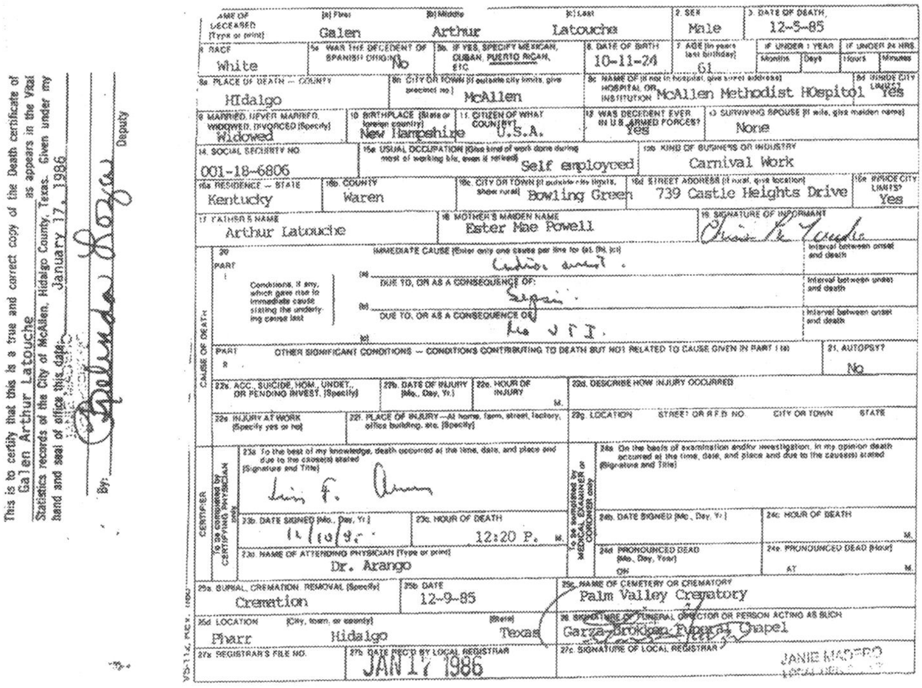

This is to certify that this is a true and correct copy of the Death certificate of Galen Arthur Latouche as appears in the Vital Statistics records of the City of McAllen, Hidalgo County, Texas. Given under my hand and seal of office this date January 17, 1986

By: Deputy

1. Name of Deceased (a) First / (b) Middle / (c) Last	Galen / Arthur / Latouche
2. Sex	Male
3. Date of Death	12-5-85
4. Race	White
5a. Was the decedent of Spanish origin?	No
6. Date of Birth	10-11-24
7. Age (in years last birthday)	61
8a. Place of Death — County	HIdalgo
8b. City or Town	McAllen
8c. Name of Hospital or Institution	McAllen Methodist HOspitol
8d. Inside City Limits?	Yes
9. Married, Never Married, Widowed, Divorced	Widowed
10. Birthplace	New Hampshire
11. Citizen of What Country	U.S.A.
12. Was Decedent Ever in U.S. Armed Forces?	Yes
13. Surviving Spouse	None
14. Social Security No.	001-18-6806
15a. Usual Occupation	Self employed
15b. Kind of Business or Industry	Carnival Work
16a. Residence — State	Kentucky
16b. County	Waren
16c. City or Town	Bowling Green
16d. Street Address	739 Castle Heights Drive
16e. Inside City Limits?	Yes
17. Father's Name	Arthur Latouche
18. Mother's Maiden Name	Ester Mae Powell
20. Part I (a) Immediate Cause	Cardiac arrest
(b) Due to, or as a consequence of	Sepsis
(c) Due to, or as a consequence of	[illegible]
21. Autopsy?	No
23c. Hour of Death	12:20 P. M.
23d. Name of Attending Physician	Dr. Arango
25a. Burial, Cremation, Removal	Cremation
25b. Date	12-9-85
25c. Name of Cemetery or Crematory	Palm Valley Crematory
25d. Location (City, town, or county) / State	Pharr / Hidalgo / Texas
26. Funeral Director or Person Acting as Such	Garza-Brookman Funeral Chapel
27b. Date Rec'd by Local Registrar	JAN 17 1986
27c. Signature of Local Registrar	JANIE MADERO

Biography of My Mother, Mary Maxine Roome

My mother was one of three sisters and was the child of Charles Phillip Roome and Ruth Juanita Whipple.

Both my father and mother had several children, but due to conflicts their marriage ended in 1952. My father moved to Texas and remarried and had two children while traveling throughout Texas as a photographer.

My mother wasn't as fortunate; she suffered from depression and was soon arrested for passing fraudulent checks and sentenced to the Indiana Women's Prison.

While my mother was in prison, she became acquainted with another inmate named Frances Lingenfield, whom I had the pleasure of meeting during my early twenties.

Frances Lingenfield told me that she actually assisted in my mother's escape from prison, using the home of her parents on Georgetown Road in Indianapolis, Indiana.

According to both Frances Lingenfield and Galen La Touché, my mother fled to Texas to once again be with my father.

With the excitement of being together once again, both my father and mother became involved in a sexual encounter, and my mother became pregnant—with me.

Out of jealousy, my father's second wife had notified the authorities of my mother's whereabouts, and she was soon apprehended and returned to the Indiana Women's Prison to complete her sentence.

It was during this time when my mother was taken to the Indiana University Coleman Hospital, where I was to be born prematurely (four pounds, fourteen ounces) on October 15, 1953, at 8:51 a.m.

Since the feuding hadn't stopped between my father and my mother's family, it was rumored that she told my mother that I had died shortly after emergency cesarean section, in hopes that my mother would write my father and tell him of my death, to prevent either of them from finding me after her release.

Prior to my mother's apprehension, it was believed that my birth was not only to spite her family, but arrangements were supposedly made to have me returned to my father in Texas or to his family in New Hampshire, where I was to stay until my mother's release from prison.

Needless to say, I became a ward of the state, known as infant La Touché, while my father continued traveling with carnivals and attending 4-H fairs throughout Texas.

After my mother was released from prison, she married Charles W. Maves, a shoe salesman in Indianapolis, and she soon gave birth to Charlene Ruth Maves before she and Charles divorced.

During this time my mother married a man named John Morgan before she died from lung cancer in Methodist Hospital, Indianapolis, Indiana, at the age of forty-four.

Family Record

NAME: MARY MAXINE ROOME

BIRTH: AUGUST 6, 1927

GENDER: F

PLACE: CONNERSVILLE, INDIANA

RACE: CAUCASIAN

MARRIAGE: AUGUST 30, 1947

PLACE: INDIANAPOLIS, INDIANA

AGE: 20 YEARS

DEATH: FEBRUARY 2, 1972

AGE: 44 YEARS

INTMT: DALE CEMENTERY

PLACE: CONNERSVILLE, INDIANA

FATHER: CHARLES PHILLIP ROOME

MOTHER: RUTH JEANETTA WHIPPLE

My Mother's Death Certificate

Indiana University Medical Center

My Birth Room Record

Certificate of Birth

Certificate of Birth

No.113 53-091534

This Certifies that according to the records of the Indiana State Board of Health

Name David Michael La Touche

Was born in the state of Indiana on October 15, 1953

Child of Galen A. & Mary M. La Touche

Birthplace of father New Hampshire Birthplace of mother Indiana

Record was filed November 1953

1s

NOT VALID UNLESS MACHINE SIGNED WITH MULTI-COLORED RIBBON

Foster Home

Several months after my birth I was placed into a foster home where it was decided that I would be given the name of David as my first name and Michael as my middle name.

For several months my foster mother's son had gotten jealous because his mother had repeatedly taken me to the hospital. That may have caused an incident at a city park located at Roosevelt and Olney Streets, where I was hit twice with a swing and knocked down.

According to reports, I had gotten up and was knocked down again; at no time did I ever lose consciousness, but a defibrillator had to be used to keep me from going into further shock just before being transported to Marion County General Hospital on Sunday, June 16, 1957.

After my discharge from the hospital, my hyperactivity worsened to where my behavior wasn't acceptable, so I was taken to the Marion County Children's Guardian Home when I was six years old.

Marion County Children's Guardian Home

Upon walking into the dormitory, I noticed every kid was in bed, either sleeping or with their heads covered, and it wasn't yet six o'clock at night. It was still light outside, and I was instructed to change into my pajamas and get into bed.

I wasn't able to just lie there and fall asleep right away; the den mother came out of a room and began whipping me across my arms and shoulders with a rubber seal that had been removed from the window screens.

After several days went by, I soon became a victim of circumstances.

My size made it easy for other children to push me around and make fun of me by calling me names.

Because of my disability, I was often used as a punching bag. I soon became acquainted with Franklin Lee Parker, and like myself, Frank had many disadvantages that caused him to be unhappy; he had been abruptly taken away from his family during his younger years and was placed into the orphanage home by the welfare department.

On numerous occasions, I became fond of a hallway closet that Frank would lock me into using a combination padlock; it would help keep me out of harm's way.

Though it was tough for me to understand, Frank did care in his own way. As kids would often do, both Frank and I made a pact to the end.

Picture of Mr. and Mrs. William S. Banks.
Picture taken during visitation.

Foster Home

Until my thirteenth year, I was always either at the foster home or the orphanage.

I experienced many frustrations, especially when I learned during my eighth year that my foster mother wasn't my real mother, but she did have hopes of adopting me.

After many questions, I didn't feel right about being adopted and I soon wanted to know who my real family was.

Both my foster mother and the Marion County Welfare Department social worker made promises to actually locate and reintroduce me to my biological family.

After time went by, I soon learned as a child that promises were lies because they were soon to be broken, in hopes that I would eventually forget about wanting to know about my real family.

Needless to say, I soon became frustrated, and as a child not knowing where to go or who to ask for help, I started to run away from the foster home. Because of this, I was taken back to the Marion County Children's Guardian Home.

Indpls Public School Photo

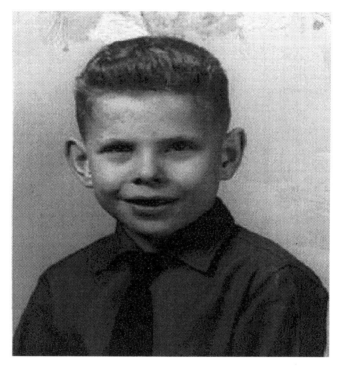

Picture taken during 1960–61 at seven years old.

Indianapolis Public
School Records

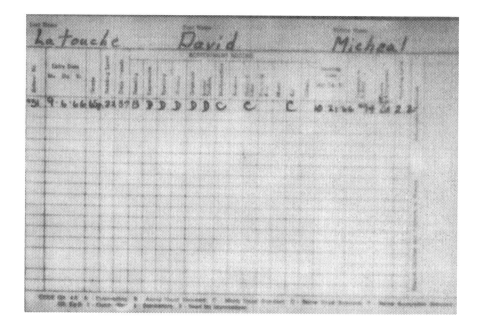

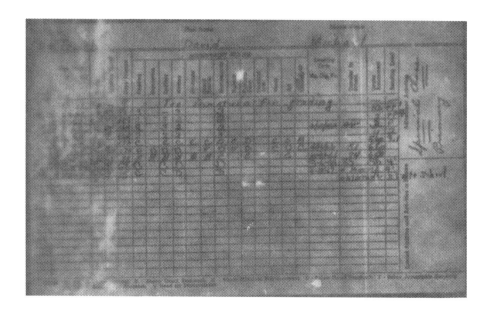

Juvenile Detention Center

I was eventually taken to the juvenile detention center in 1966 after becoming a chronic runaway.

After several days in detention, I was taken to court. Upon entering I had noticed my foster mother sitting nearby, and I asked to be seated next to her.

As I looked around the courtroom, I noticed a large black man sitting behind a desk wearing a black robe, and if you were told stories when you were small about the bogeyman, it was soon to be true.

I became frighten and scared, so I clenched my mother's arm while crying in fear of the boogey man, because he was going to get me!

I was soon returned to solitary confinement where I was being kept and after a few weeks had gone by, I was allowed visitation from my foster mother.

Often times, when in despair, my foster mother would always find a way to cheer a gloomy day, and the key was, with this kid, a bag of candied apples and tootsie rolls.

The candied apples and Tootsie Roll's lit up my eyes like a kid in a candy store!

Foster Home

They were soon eaten and what candy was left was taken away after I was returned to solitary.

After several months I was returned to the foster home, and often my foster father would play the villain, especially when coming home after drinking and boasting with his buddies at the bar.

I remember he would load everyone in the car for a family drive while he was intoxicated.

Often times, he wasn't bashful about showing his anger and often times, he would drive by the juvenile detention center with the car door opened, closest to me hoping that I would fall out while he drove off.

When this didn't happen, he would grab me and try to throw me through the door. Once we returned back home, he would send all of the kids upstairs for a while, but instead, I hid in a closet in the next room.

After hearing a loud noise, I quietly came out of the closet and, on my hands and knees came around the corner using the recliner that my foster father used to keep hidden.

As I peeked around, I noticed that the bookcase had been knocked over, books were lying throughout the living room and my foster mother was laying face down on the floor, bleeding from being cut.

My foster father stood over her with both fists doubled yelling, "Why don't you get rid of "David"?

I jumped straight up from where I was hiding and yelled "NO", and just before my foster father tried to grab me, I ran as fast as I could out the kitchen door and I hid under the outside porch.

From my safe place, I could watch my foster father, through the cracks in the boards, as he came raging outside to try and find me.

As time went by and my foster mother would step outside to call me to come back inside, I could see the door open or close looking up through the cracks in the porch floor.

Not knowing if my foster father had left to return to the bar.

I was still afraid to go back inside for fear of what would happen next.

When my foster mother would stand on the porch crying, I would cry with her until it was safe to return back inside.

This wasn't the first nor the last time, my father would attack my mother, and soon after the attack I was eventually taken back to the orphanage home where I learned that my friend Franklin Lee Parker had been taken to the Muscatatuck.

Marion County Childrens Guardian Home

Not realizing the Marion County Welfare Department had already failed from petitioning the court to have me committed to Muscatatuck, I requested to speak with my caseworker Bradley Bingman to see if I could be reacquainted with my friend Franklin Lee Parker.

This finally gave the Marion County Children's Guardian Home and the Welfare Department the advantage needed for them to have me committed to Muscatatuck State School.

I soon became a ward of the state where I was taken from the orphanage home on February 28, 1967.

I voluntarily signed a form to be admitted to the Muscatatuck State School and Training Center during my thirteenth year where I was placed in a state mental institution where I experience many frustrations of not knowing who, where, or was my natural family.

Picture taken at age 13 Years

Muscatatuck State Hospital And Training Center

Building 4

Ward A   Upstairs

Ward B   Downstairs

I was taken to Muscatatuck State School and Training Center from the Marion County Children's Guardian Home (Orphanage Home) on April 18, 1967 because I was considered to be mentally retarded.

Due to my previous education prior to coming to Muscatatuck I was asked to attend a dedication ceremony that meant meeting with the previous superintendent, and receiving a very large book with instructions that it is taken back to the ward where I was staying.

The dedication ceremony also meant Muscatatuck State School and Training Center became Muscatatuck State Hospital and Training Center.

Shortly after being admitted Muscatatuck, I started to experience a combination of chills and warmth as if I were experiencing regret.

The most traumatic experience I had is when I saw a friend fall to his death from playing on a second floor balcony while I was being brought in from visitation from visiting with Deanna Kress Kelly and her family in Tell City Indiana just minutes before I walked around the corner seeing the upper part of his body covered in blood.

After seeing my friend Herman Hamm lying there with his face covered in his blood, I could see the fear in his eyes and I knew then that life could be taken away without warning.

There was a funeral service for him and after talking with the hospital Chaplin, I was baptized at the age of sixteen years on January 4, 1970.

Even as a troubled youngster, I had always wanted to attend church because to me, learning something as great as what Christ can do for others made me feel for that moment there was not a care in the world for me to worry about.

Baptismal Certificate

We do Certify

THAT, ACCORDING TO THE ORDINANCE OF
OUR LORD JESUS CHRIST, WE DID ADMINISTER TO

David Michael La Touche

WHO WAS BORN AT Indianapolis, (marion) Indiana

ON October 15,   A.D. 1953

THE SACRAMENT OF

Holy Baptism

WITH WATER,
IN THE NAME OF THE FATHER, AND OF
THE SON, AND OF THE HOLY GHOST

IN Muscatatuck State Hospital And Training Center

Butlerville, Indiana

ON January 04,   A.D. 1970

THEREBY MAKING him A MEMBER OF CHRIST, THE CHILD OF GOD,
AND AN INHERITOR OF THE KINGDOM OF HEAVEN.

PARENTS Galen Arthur La Touche

Mary Maxine Roome

SPONSORS _____

(SIGNED) _Charles E. Chambers, Chaplain_

No. 110 M-B Co. Printed in U.S.A.

51

Picture of Muscatatuck Bldg 10

Building	10
Ward A	Downstairs
Ward B	Upstairs

This caused me to become interested in reading about the history of the institution and there were occasions when I would be asked if I would enjoy acting as an escort, taking groups around the buildings, and grounds, giving a an interpretation and a brief explanation of the different age groups.

Cemetery

Chapel

One Sunday, I decided to not to attend church service (with someone else), and after church was over; both of us were taken in to solitary on December 2, 1973.

I didn't quite understand why someone would be locked up until the next day for not attending church services, by a person who also was to have sexual relations with some of the other patients.

After about an hour, the door opened and I was asked to return to my unit, were I soon received a surprise visit from my foster mother.

While visiting with my foster mother I was told that she had brought me a bicycle but it was to be locked up until after my detention was over.

Meanwhile she kept me occupied with the games, playing cards she brought for me including candied apples and cookies.

After sitting at the band stand area next to the school building, I noticed one of the other boys riding his bike nearby as he had done with other families to report back to the staff.

I pleaded with my foster mother, could we go somewhere else, so we moved to a park area where I had this picture taken.

Picture At Muscatatuck Park

The reason why I didn't look happy in this picture, is because they young boy who was riding his bike over by the band stand, also showed up at the park to were I couldn't enjoy my visit with my family.

After the visit was over, I was taken back to my unit, where I was criticized because I moved with my family from the bandstand to the park over by the administration building before I was taken back in to solitary.

The next day, I was allowed to go o work and school before returning back to my unit. As I walked in to my unit, I told by one of the other boys, everybody went through my things and thrown on my bed. What wasn't thrown on my bed was eaten or broken.

After awhile I was invited to go home with my foster mother to her new home in Gosport Indiana to spend the Christmas Holiday Season in hopes to have me come live with her again.

However, too much time had passed to where I wasn't the same little boy that my mother once knew.

By the time everybody had again told me about my foster father leaving my foster mother and her children, these stories had brought back such horrifying memories to where I eventually had to be taken back to the Muscatatuck State Hospital.

Cardinal Cottage

Fort Wayne State Hospital And Training Center

After several months, I was transferred to the Fort Wayne State Hospital and Training Center, August 1971.

I ended up being hospitalized because of two bullies who had a habit of putting things into people's milk causing them to experience stomach cramps, which caused me to be taken to Lutheran Hospital for an emergency appendectomy.

Following this incident, I learned that no matter what was said, I wasn't going to have any peace because of the two bullies, so I began to run away and I was eventually returned to Muscatatuck on March 13, 1972.

Oak Cottage

In 1974, I went to Columbus, Indiana, and watched a school play called "West Side Story" where I started talking with one of the cast members.

I soon found myself being introduced to his parents. I must have made a good impression because their son came to Muscatatuck State Hospital to visit with me, and after the first visit he was allowed to take me to his home in Columbus, Indiana to stay with him and his family at Grandview Lake for the weekends.

After a couple of visits, the Quick Family wanted to sponsor me to attend a new program that that was developing and asked if I would be interested in coming to Columbus to be trained in a sheltered workshop.

One of the caseworkers at Muscatatuck was not in favor of me being sponsored, and so I rebelled by saying that I had already spent over seven years in Muscatatuck.

I really hadn't been properly taught anything except learning what it is to be institutionalized, making hospital beds, washing dishes, grounds keeping, and attending special education classes.

After I reminded him I had already achieved a fifth grade education level he began to intimidate and threaten me by saying if I didn't make it with the sheltered workshop program I would be brought back to Muscatatuck and he would make my life miserable.

I said to him he already had! In August 1974, my social worker from Muscatatuck State Hospital drove me to Columbus, Indiana, where I stayed in a group home on Camelot Lane where I attended a sheltered workshop.

Developmental Services Inc

After about ten months, I felt I was being pressured by one of the program directors that caused me to develop manic explosive disorders toward others and I was taken back to Muscatatuck.

As I was riding back, my social worker informed me that after two weeks, I could write a letter to the superintendent of Muscatatuck State Hospital and Training Center requesting my discharge, but I was told not to say anything about this conversation with him, and even though I agreed not to say anything, I did ask him if he could be with me during the meeting with the superintendent, and he said yes.

On June 10, 1975, I wrote a letter to the superintendent of the hospital requesting my discharge.

The superintendent had already assumed that my caseworker had influenced me to write the letter requesting my discharge.

The superintendent asked me to step into the other room while he abruptly became verbally aggressive with my social worker.

According to the latest psychological report dated August 25, 1974, my full scale Intelligence Quotient showed 85% which placed me within the normal range of measured intelligence.

This score exceeded the guidelines of someone being held for hospitalization in a state hospital within the State of Indiana the superintendent was forced to grant me my discharge after eight years, two months, and six days, on June 26, 1975 where I was taken to Indianapolis Indiana.

Certificate Of Discharge

M R - 11

CERTIFICATE OF DISCHARGE

FROM

MUSCATATUCK STATE HOSPITAL and TRAINING CENTER

To: Clerk of the Circuit Court

Marion County

Indianapolis, Indiana

In compliance with the requirements of Chapter 338 of the Acts of 1955,
(Burns 1955 Cumulative Pocket Supplement to Vol. V. Pt. II. 22-4240 to
22-4244 inclusive), the Superintendent of Muscatatuck State Hospital and
Training Center hereby notifies the Clerk of the _____ Marion

_____ County Circuit Court that __David Michael LaTouche__
(Name of Patient)
committed to this institution on ____January 15, 1964____ , under
(Date)
___X63-336___ , and whose address at the time of commitment was
(Cause Number)

__Indianapolis, Indiana__ was discharged from this

institution on ___June 26, 1975___ . The aforementioned individual was
(Date)
discharged to the custody of _____ "Self" _____ whose
(Name of person or "self")
address is __252 North Koehne, Indianapolis, Indiana__ . In my

opinion the aforementioned ____David Michael LaTouche____ is no
(Name of Individual)
longer a mentally ill person within the meaning of the statute.

_____
Superintendent

Muscatatuck State Hospital and Training Center

State of Indiana   }
                     } SS:
County of Jennings   }

Subscribed and sworn to before me this 26 day of June , 19 75.

_____
Notary Public

My commission expires 9-20-78

Testimonial

"A long time ago ... David was my little brother. I guess he's still my little brother but time has allowed him to become bigger that I am.

Years ago when I came home on leave from the Marine Corps the first morning I woke to find David ... A little kid then ... Had opened a carton of lucky strike cigarettes ... And had them torn up and scattered all over the bedroom floor ... What mess ...?

I became furious until I looked in to his sweet smiling face and listen to him tell me how proud he was of himself for helping me unpack! How long could I stay mad ...? Not very long!

In the 1950's I took the train from Indianapolis to Chicago and then on to Los Angeles ... After I had reached Los Angeles I traveled by bus to Camp Pendleton. Several days later David was found walking along the train tracks.

David tried to explain to who ever found him that his big brother had taken the train to California and was going to walk those tracks until he got to California where he would find me!

Stephen Banks
Brent, PA

Family Record

NAME: <u>DAVID MICHAEL LATOUCHE</u>

BIRTH: <u>OCTOBER 15 1953</u>

GENDER: <u>M</u>

PLACE: <u>INDIANAPOLIS, INDIANA</u>

RACE: <u>CAUCASIAN</u>

BAPTISM: <u>JANUARY 4, 1970</u>

PLACE: <u>MUSCATATUCK STATE HOSPITAL</u>

AGE: <u>16 YEARS</u>

DEATH: _____

AGE: _____

INTMT: <u>TRINITY EPISCOPAL CHURCH</u>

PLACE: <u>INDIANAPOLIS INDIANA</u>

FATHER: <u>GALEN ARTHUR LATOUCHE</u>

MOTHER: <u>MARY MAXINE ROOME</u>

Educational

00/00/0000	EDUCATIONSCHOOL	IQ
12/19/1959	Indpls Public School #9	58
10/21/1988	Indpls Public School #74	
05/00/1962	Indpls Public School #85	59
11/19/1965	Indpls Public School #51	64
09/24/1985	Developmental Services Inc	85

Housing Locations

00/00/0000	HOUSING LOCATIONS	COMMENTS
10/15/1953	Indiana University Coleman Hospital	Birth Record
00/00/1954	Foster Home	Indianapolis
00/00/0000	Children's Guardian Home	Indianapolis
00/00/0000	Juvenile Detention Center	Indianapolis
00/00/0000	Muscatatuck State School	Butlerville
00/00/0000	Foster Home	Vincennes
08/00/1971	Fort Wayne State Hospital	Fort Wayne
05/02/1975	Muscatatuck State Hospital	Butlerville
00/00/1974	Developmental Services Inc	Columbus
06/18/1975	Goodwill Industries	Indianapolis
06/26/1975	Muscatatuck State Hospital	Discharge

Hospital Visitations

00/00/0000	HOSPITAL VISITATIONS	COMMENTS
01/19/1973	Ruth Olmstead	24-Hours
12/22/1973	Mary Banks	04-Days
06/21/1974	Barney Quick	04-Days
10/11/1974	Barney Quick	Out-to-Dinner

Resources

CEMETERY RECORDS	EXTENSION	TELEPHONE
Dale Cemetery 801 N. Gregg Road Connersville, IN 47331	Curator	(856) 787-5222

BIRTH AND DEATH RECORDS	EXTENSION	TELEPHONE
New Hampshire Dept of State Division of Vital Records Adm 71 South Fruit Street Concord, NH 03301-2410	Information Genealogy Vault Facsimile	(800) 851-3345 (603) 271-4650 (603) 271-3447
Indiana State Department of Health 2 N. Meridian Street Indianapolis, IN 46204-3021	Vital Statistics Facsimile	(317) 233-2700 (317) 591-5324

HOSPITAL RECORDS	EXTENSION	TELEPHONE
Indiana State Archives	Curator's Office	(317) 591-5222
6440 East 30th Street	Curator's Facsimile	(317) 591-5324
Indianapolis, IN 46219-1007		

LIBRARY RESOURCES	EXTENSION	TELEPHONE
Indiana State Library	Switchboard	(317) 232-3675
140 N. Senate Avenue	Genealogy Section	(317) 232-3689
Indianapolis, IN 45204-2296	Facsimile	(317) 232-3728
Nat'l Archives/Records Administration	Information	(800) 827-4898
700 Pennsylvania Avenue, N.W.	Genealogy Dept	(202) 501-5500
Washington, DC 20408-0002	Facsimile	(202) 501-5402

Family Record Form

NAME: _____   SPOUSE: _____
BIRTH: _____   BIRTH: _____
PLACE: _____   PLACE: _____
SEX: _____   SEX: _____

BAPTISM: _____ BAPTISM: _____
PLACE _____   PLACE: _____
AGE: _____   AGE: _____

MILITARY: _____ MILITARY: _____
ENTERED: _____ ENTERED: _____
DISCHARGED: _____ DISCHARGED: _____
RANK: _____   RANK: _____

MARRIAGE: _____ MARRIAGE: _____
PLACE: _____   PLACE: _____
AGE: _____   AGE: _____

DEATH: _____   DEATH: _____
CAUSE: _____   CAUSE: _____
PLACE: _____   PLACE: _____
AGE: _____   AGE: _____

INTMT: _____ INTMT: _____
PLACE: _____ PLACE: _____

FATHER: _____ FATHER: _____
MOTHER: _____ MOTHER: _____

I personally created this form to help me better
understand in researching the individual.

Author's Note

Now that I'm an adult I feel that I am still not free from the torment. I am constantly reminded of the recurring moments of my earlier years as a child through my nightmares and having been told what others believe that I am incompetent or incapable of ever being someone significant.

DAVID MICHAEL LATOUCHE
Author

Printed in the United States
By Bookmasters